Published by
Lion Publishing plc
Sandy Lane West, Oxford, England
ISBN 0 7459 3334 3
Albatross Books Pty Ltd
PO Box 320, Sutherland, NSW 2232, Australia
ISBN 0 7324 1291 9

First edition 1995
10 9 8 7 6 5 4 3 2 1 0

A catalogue record for this book is available
from the British Library

Printed and bound in Malaysia

Glimpses of Nature

Unusual perspectives on the natural world

DAVID BOAG

A LION BOOK

Introduction

Ever since I was 'knee high to a grasshopper' I have marvelled at the natural world. As a young boy I would go into our garden, in the London suburbs, and capture scores of ladybirds and put them into jam jars. I collected butterflies and all kinds of beautiful specimens, not because I wanted to harm them, but because I had a fascination with all living things.

However, it is not possible to collect samples of wildlife without destroying them, so later I began to use a camera to do my 'collecting'. I have now been a professional wildlife photographer for several years, and I count it a privilege to spend my life doing what I most enjoy.

It was when I started taking photographs that I first noticed the incredible patterns in nature. Until then I had concentrated my enthusiasm on studying animals and plants. Looking through the camera lens, however, I noticed forms and shapes that fired my imagination. Suddenly I was looking at things in a new way, and I wanted to record them on film.

I still spend most of my time photographing mammals, birds, insects and plants. But I cannot take a country ramble without noticing at least a few interesting patterns. Of course they are not there simply for me to enjoy; they are for everyone with the eyes and the enthusiasm to discover them.

Fern

Some time ago, I was working on a photographic book about a large private garden that was connected to a country manor. It was no ordinary garden. A walk through the grounds would first take me past an old thatched building that served as a range of garden sheds. Next came the rose garden, where the crazy paving paths converged on a sundial that was surrounded by clouds of blue lavender. A maze of yew hedges and flower borders then led on to an orchard of all kinds of fruit trees, and this in turn sloped down to a bubbling stream which you could cross on a little footbridge. The path along the stream followed a delightful walk through woods and then the trees parted to reveal a lake. Graceful willow trees bent to touch the water here, and in the summer yellow flag irises surrounded the lake in a blaze of glory. Finally, a great lawn swept up to the grand house and in the centre of the lawn was a statue that was surrounded by ferns.

The owners of the property were always very interested in my work and we would often chat about the new discoveries I had made in the grounds – nesting birds or the leafy lair of a sleepy toad.

After several months I showed them some of my pictures. To my surprise, the lady of the house asked, 'Could you spare the time to show me round the garden one day?' How strange, I thought. Surely she knew the garden as well as I did, having lived there for many years? 'You see so much more than I do,' she explained.

A few days later we enthused together about the things I pointed out as we walked around the grounds. 'The problem I have,' she said, 'is that I see it every day, so I don't bother to take the time to enjoy it.'

And I realized that we all have things we take for granted, because they have become too familiar.

Dragonfly Lace

When a butterfly or dragonfly first emerges, its wings are limp and crumpled. Then, miraculously, fluid is pumped into the veins and very slowly they expand. After a while, the delicate wings of gossamer lace are dry and at last the insect is able to take to the air.

The design of an insect's wing is remarkable. Each one is extremely light, but because some insects have to fold them away, their wings also need to be collapsible. The wings of many insects therefore look distinctly weak and fragile, but in fact they are very strong.

When I was in business it was clear that the strong and powerful personalities forced their way to the top of the promotion ladder, while the quiet and apparently weaker people were left behind. I can remember the same sort of principle in the playground at school where the strong were respected and the weak rejected.

God has a habit of turning things around! The Bible says that 'the first shall be last and the last, first' and that the strength of God is 'made perfect in our weakness'.

A dragonfly's wings may look weak and can easily be crushed or torn, but when in flight they are very strong. The strength is in the design. God accepts and loves the weak, because they rely on a strength which he gives them: an inner strength, designed by God.

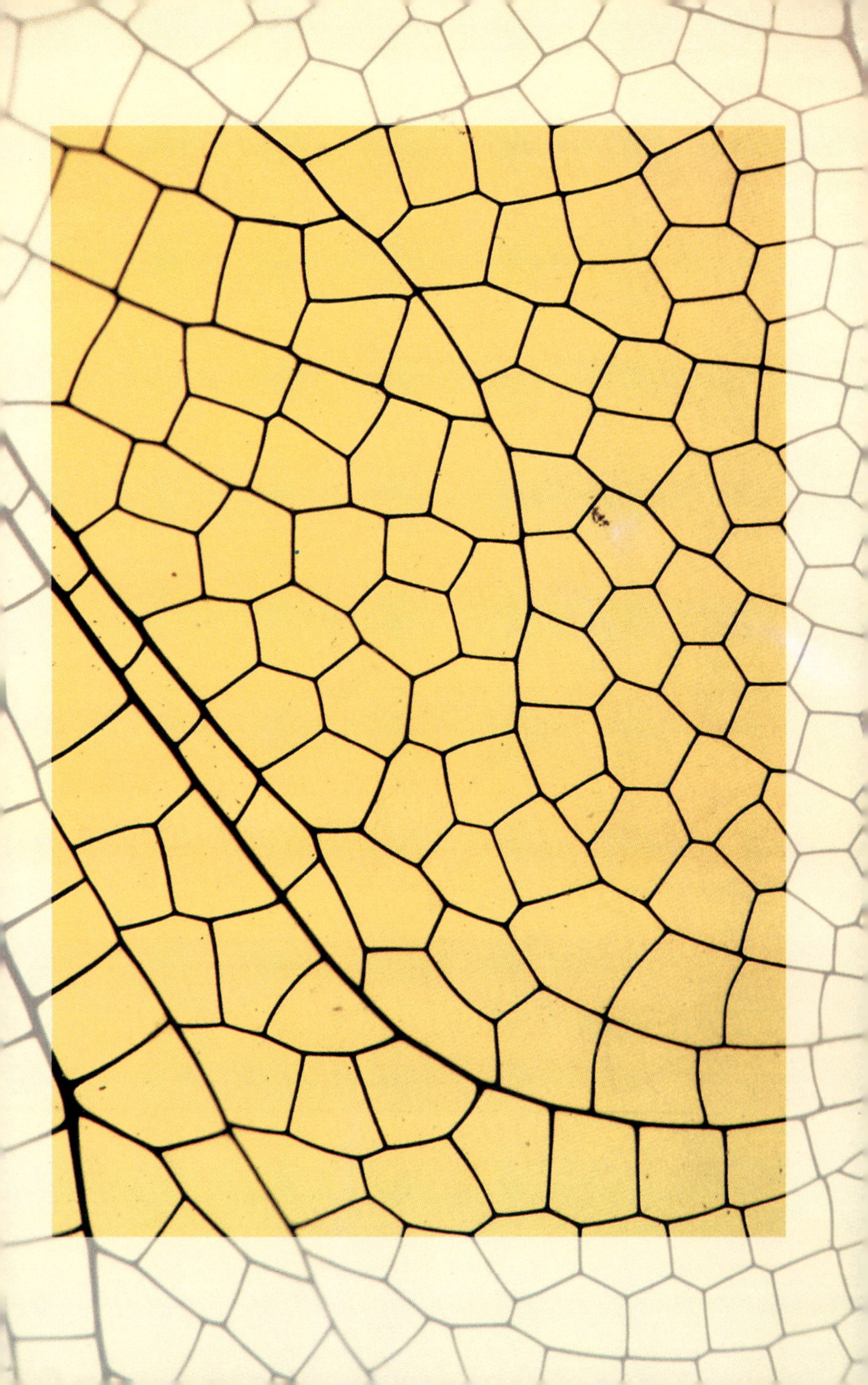

Daisies

What do you think of my lawn? 'Not very good, it's full of weeds,' some of you would say!

But that's a matter of opinion. Your weeds are my daisies – wild flowers that are beautiful in their simplicity. At least that's the argument I put to my wife when she comments on the state of the lawn.

It's funny how we pick and choose the things we find acceptable. Plants that we enjoy in the countryside we call weeds in the garden. I have heard weeds described as 'the right plant growing in the wrong place' and I suppose that's true. But who decides?

Sometimes, human beings are made to feel that they are in the wrong place at the wrong time. Some even live out their lives feeling unwanted or out of place. But who decides?

God is the creator and only he can really decide. He sees beauty in each of us and has chosen to put us where we are. No plant is a weed in God's garden.

Butterfly Wings

Do you know how many scales it takes to create the complete and extraordinary pattern on the wing of a butterfly? I have worked out that there are over 13,500 scales in this photograph alone, and that is only one section of the whole.

Just like stitches in an intricate embroidery, each scale is important. A scale on its own may be small and insignificant, but bring all the scales together and the beauty of the small tortoiseshell's wing is truly amazing.

As individuals we can only demonstrate a tiny part of God's design for the world. Yet because each individual has different gifts and abilities, we create a pattern together that is unique. When we also devote those gifts and abilities to serving God in the world around us, the pattern becomes more beautiful still. For then we can represent a bigger part of God to those around us.

Blossom

Spring arrives in different ways for each of us: primroses unfurling to adorn a woodland glade, or birds beginning to nest; catkins, and daffodils bursting into bloom, new buds appearing on the trees: they all indicate spring in their own ways. I particularly love the clouds of blossom on the hawthorn bush, where delicate white blooms contrast with the hard, sharp thorns.

Once the plants are active in the spring, insects too can begin to flourish, feeding either on the new growth or from the fresh flowers. Plants rely on insects to do the work of pollination; without insects, plants would be unable to reproduce and the next generation would be lost. But without the blossom insects would die for lack of food.

Wherever we look in the natural world we can see the interaction between species. One thing relies on another. In the same way, God created people so that he could love them and they could love him. He relies on us to show his love to others, and we can rely upon him to be with us when we need his help.

Adder

Often during a lecture, I project a series of beautiful flower photographs onto the screen. Then I shock my audience by unexpectedly displaying a close-up picture of an adder. It never fails to get a reaction! Many people respond by showing extra interest, while others show their dislike – even though they cannot take their eyes from the picture and are eager to hear more about it. However, there are always a few who look away or close their eyes until the next picture appears.

We often see and hear things in the news that we find disturbing. Perhaps we see children suffering in a war-torn part of the world, or starving families or people living in 'cardboard cities'. How do we react to these shocking realities?

I admit that I find it very difficult to watch such things. They upset me and I would rather leave the room and make a cup of tea. I am not unlike those people who turn their heads away from the sight of the adder. But I am wrong!

How much better the world is when our distress becomes concern, our concern becomes compassion and our compassion becomes prayer and action.

Autumn Leaf on Duckweed

For several years I have used this photograph when lecturing about river life. The point I try to make is that nature provides us with delightful contrasts, if we look at it carefully enough.

On one occasion I enthused about the wonderful colours, seen here, on the surface of a pond – the contrast between the burnt-orange of the maple leaf and the fresh green of the duckweed. During the interval someone came up to me and, referring to the photograph, philosophized about the contrast between life and death.

At the time I chatted amiably and said that I understood. But as I was driving home it occurred to me that to compare life and death in this way implies a complete lack of purpose. How depressing it is if we believe we merely end our lives like rotting, dry leaves.

Jesus Christ gave people hope for the future. He showed them that they are more than just leaves falling from a tree. For in death, we can look forward to meeting our creator in a new life, and it will be more splendid and perfect than anything we have ever known.

Fungi

Fungi are largely made up of mycelia, consisting of microscopic threadlike hyphae. For most of the time this curious vegetative matter is hidden within rotting wood or dung, or under the soil. We tend to assume that fallen branches and old trees decay because they are dead, but this process of degeneration is often the work of fungi – which we may never see. Without fungi and other hidden organisms and tiny creatures nothing could be recycled into the miraculous systems we call life.

Recently I heard someone say that most fungi are active during the autumn. Although it is true that the majority of species of fungi produce their fruiting bodies at that time of year, the statement is not strictly accurate. Fungi are active throughout much of the year; it's just that for most of the time we are unaware of their existence. We tend to take for granted the work that fungi do and we don't notice them until they produce something visible.

Some human beings escape our attention too, even though they may do critically important work. All too often we concentrate on obvious results, and judge people by what they produce. But there are others who have a different approach to life and get on with a task unseen and often ignored. It is a shame that unless their good deeds are made visible, such people are rarely encouraged.

Gannets

During the breeding season gannets have a strong desire to nest in huge colonies where they are close to others of their own kind. However, gannets still maintain a miniature territory, the size of which is determined by the length of their necks and beaks. As each bird sits on its nest, it constantly strikes out to defend its patch as if not trusting its neighbours. As a result the nests are evenly spaced throughout the colony. The expression 'so near and yet so far' is well illustrated by the thousands of gannets that gather together to nest in this way.

Human beings often behave in a similar manner, especially when our emotions are at stake. We feel the desire to share our worries, our disappointments or our pain and to be close to someone so that they may understand how we feel. But we often dare to go only so far, just in case others don't understand and we end up feeling rejected.

Sometimes even our best friends let us down but God won't – he understands and cares. Self-protective measures are naturally very useful from time to time. But we don't always benefit from emulating the gannet, for we have a greater strength than we may know. God is never far away.

Grasses

The grass crackled under my feet and the pond was locked beneath a thick layer of ice. Twigs that had borne fresh new leaves only a few months ago were bare and brittle to touch. Everything around me seemed brown and naked, and it was so cold that I couldn't help wondering if spring would ever come again. Underneath, of course, I knew it would – it always does, and I remembered God's promise, in the Bible, that the harvest, too, would never fail.

As I thought of that promise, it occurred to me that harvest *does* fail for people in famine-stricken parts of the world. Sometimes it doesn't just fail once, but time and time again. Is God's promise not being fulfilled?

The problem is not with God, it is with us: 80 per cent of the world's wealth is in the hands of 20 per cent of the world's population. Although the harvest does fail in some areas of the world, overall there is more than enough to go around. We often pray, 'Give us this day our daily bread' – but who else is praying that prayer while we are eating their portion of the harvest?

It is so difficult to know how to help, but I think it may be a start if we acknowledge how privileged we are. Instead of complaining of the cold in winter and the heat in summer, let's turn our complaints into gratitude. Then let's turn our gratitude into action, move forward and share what we have.

Water

We do not find a glass of water very impressive to look at. Water is so much part of our life. But think about all the different aspects of water. We are used to it as a liquid, but we are also surrounded by water in the form of vapour. While clouds are easily visible, the vapour which creates the humidity in our atmosphere we can't see at all.

We also know water as ice. Inside our homes, our freezers have mundane ice cubes, but outside, from our skies, ice crystals fall as magical, intricate snowflakes, or fierce sleet or hail. The countryside can be transformed by brilliant white frosts decorating the trees, while ponds and puddles freeze into solid blocks. On other surfaces too, frozen droplets create patterns of ice crystals. Water is also vital to all forms of organic life.

There are so many aspects of water. There are also many aspects of God. It is comfortable to think of God as a gentle father, but we need, as well, to think of some of his other attributes. We must not forget justice, power, mercy, holiness and creativity.

Water takes many forms but its fundamental make-up is always the same. So it is with God, and we can take security from the fact that 'God is love' whatever aspect of him is revealed.

Fallen Leaves

Each year I run a weekend course teaching photography of the natural world. At some point during the weekend, I suggest that each person takes a piece of rope about four metres long and ties one end to their ankle and the other to a tree in the woods. They are instructed to stay there for half an hour, with the aim of taking ten good pictures within the four-metre radius.

Before suggesting it to my pupils, however, I obviously needed to try it for myself. At first nothing was apparent and I wished that I had tied myself to a different tree where pictures might be easier to find. But after five minutes, I became resigned to the fact that I was stuck with this tree for another twenty-five minutes. Almost immediately I noticed a single leaf caught in a spider's web and I took my first photograph. Then I concentrated on some moss-covered roots, and soon the ideas and pictures began to flow. I stayed with my tree for forty minutes and took thirteen pictures. This close-up on a fallen leaf is one of them.

How often do we wish we were somewhere else or doing something different? Unfortunately, it is not until we learn to be content where we are that life looks a little brighter. We start enjoying things that only yesterday we considered boring, or didn't notice at all. We start living life to the full.

Mud

The sticky, brown mire found in estuaries is well-named by the word 'mud'. In the photograph it has been dried by the sun and the wind into a crazy-paving pattern. Where the mud is still semi-liquid, it contains more life than any other part of the land. It is full of molluscs, crustaceans, worms and other organisms, and the abundance of life is well illustrated by the thousands of birds that feed on these hidden invertebrates. However, we still screw up our noses and call it mud.

What we call each other is important. In biblical times the name someone was given portrayed something of their character, or God's purpose or promise for that person. Children use bad names to hurt each other and some adults call one another 'useless' or 'stupid'. But very often what we call someone reflects *our* attitude towards that person, rather than any intrinsic character he or she may have.

Whatever other people think of us, and whatever we think of them, it doesn't change who they are or who we are. We may be quick to judge, to form impressions. But we can't know what someone is really like, and what over many years has made them behave in the way they do. We need to get beneath the labels.

Fortunately, God knows the real us, and what is hidden within each of us. It is on that, ultimately, that we depend.

Reflections

I always think this photograph looks like a crazy television screen, where all the lines of the picture have slipped sideways and the image has become completely distorted. In a way, that is what has happened here, for these are the reflections on the surface of a pond and the rippling water has distorted the image of surrounding countryside.

On the day I took the photograph the sky was an intense blue void with the occasional fluffy white cloud – its reflection can be seen in the photograph. It was taken during autumn, and the tree nearby was clothed in wonderful seasonal colours – equally well reflected. There is even a suggestion of the dark trunk of a tree.

We are made in God's image, and so we reflect his character. Of course none of us is perfect and so we cannot possibly reflect him perfectly in the way that Jesus did when he lived. However, through the chequered reflections of our lives each of us can reflect a little of the beauty of God's character.

Perhaps we can all learn from the pond: the stiller the water, the more perfect the reflection.

Sand

On a beautiful clear day in mid-winter, I wrapped myself up against the cold and set out walking along a deserted beach. Soon I discovered some shells and took my jacket off, laying it on the ground. I had been lying there only a few moments, trying to get a very low-angle picture, when several people appeared from nowhere and began heading in my direction. Clearly they must have thought I was a dead body washed up by the tide or possibly a lunatic sun-bathing in February! No one spoke to me and they kept a respectful distance, but it was obvious my behaviour puzzled them.

A couple of days later I was on the same beach, this time pointing the camera down onto the sand. I was peering intently through the lens when a man and his dog walked within a few feet of where I was taking this photograph. I recognized the man from two days earlier (or rather I recognized his dog). Once again he gave me a quizzical glance.

Later that day I met him again but clearly he didn't recognize me. Nevertheless he ventured to say, 'Hello. I see you're a photographer,' glancing at my camera and tripod. 'The other day I saw a photographer lying flat on a beach and today I saw him again, pointing his camera at nothing but sand. What do you think he was doing?' 'Why didn't you ask him?' I replied. 'I didn't know him, so I didn't like to speak to him,' he confided. 'But you're speaking to me,' I encouraged him. 'Ah, but you look much more respectable than him,' he said.

Fallen Tree

Occasionally the strains and stresses of life leave us emotionally dry, cracked and worn out, a bit like the trunk of this tree. I once saw a sculpture where the wood-carver had chosen this type of wood, and had made clever use of both the grain and fissures in it. He had smoothed the rough edges and, using a little oil, burnished the worn-out timber until it was shining. The result was a sculpture that was both beautiful and long-lasting.

I have to admit I would rather go through life without any problems or heartaches, but I cannot help wondering what sort of person I would be if that were the case. I am sure I would find it more difficult to understand other people's problems, and would I really care about them if I had not experienced pain for myself? Surely it takes the difficult times as much as the happy ones to fashion our characters fully?

Bark

How often we use the expression, 'can't see the wood for the trees'.

A good illustration of the phrase is this photograph of the bark of a yew tree. Yew woods are now rare where I live, but I had gone one day to one of the few that remained with the express purpose of capturing the atmosphere of this strange environment. Because the canopy of the trees was so thick, this yew wood was a dark and sinister place. The fallen needles carpeted the ground to a thickness of over a foot, and nothing could grow on the dark woodland floor. There seemed to be little to capture my imagination.

I spent a long time pondering the situation and took one or two pictures. I was about to leave when I noticed the bark of the tree on which I was leaning. The photograph I took then still captures for me the shadowy atmosphere, suggesting the strength of those ancient trees.

You might say I literally couldn't see the wood for the trees – I was too involved to discover what I was really looking for!

Horse Chestnut Leaf

I sometimes feel that selecting just a small part of creation can tell us as much about a location as looking at the broad sweep of a magnificent landscape. A single horse chestnut leaf that has fallen to the ground suggests woods in autumn almost as much as a typical grand forest view. Some people, of course, merely see a dead leaf. Not everyone can find beauty or interest in this type of photography.

I hope you have enjoyed the pictures in this little book, but it would give me even greater pleasure to think that you may now discover these things for yourself. However good the photograph, nothing can beat the thrill and excitement of looking at the real thing.

Setting Sun

As a full-time wildlife photographer I have a collection of thousands of photographs. They are all filed away in a cabinet and some I have not seen for years. But select any picture from my files and I could tell you exactly when and where it was taken and a great deal more besides. Each picture brings back a flood of memories.

This picture of the setting sun's reflections on water was taken in the Scottish highlands. I had been searching for an otter all day, and had found one just as the sun was going down. I remember the excitement I felt as I stalked this glorious creature closer and closer until I was able to take my photographs. Afterwards I sat by the edge of the loch feeling elated, drinking a cup of coffee from my flask. I sat there, listening to the gulls, until it was almost too dark to see. All those memories – more, even – from one very simple picture.

Tips for Photographing Nature

Don't spend too much time on equipment and technical know-how. Think about the more creative side of photography.

Decide what aspect about a subject particularly appeals to you. It could be the detail, the size, the atmosphere or the colour of the subject. Then you'll have a clearer idea of what it is you wish to capture, and you can attempt to exaggerate that feature.

Try to use natural light. This doesn't necessarily mean bright sunshine – some of my best photographs were taken in fog. Quite often I am forced to use flash in difficult situations, when the subject is in poor light and moving too rapidly. On these occasions, I try to reproduce natural light. I try to use only one flash, and a white card to bounce some light into the heavy-shadow areas.

Above all, use your enthusiasm, enjoying the life that surrounds you!